Star Cat

Carl went to bed.
Carl's cat Dora went to bed too.

In the night ...

... Dora went prowling in the garden.

At night, Dora is Star Cat!
I am fed up with Carl's cat food!

Star Cat looks for buns to munch on.

She zooms up high!

Star Cat floats across the town.

Can she see buns in a shop?

No!

Can she see buns on a high speed train?

No! That's absurd!

Soon, she spots a stack of buns.
But a moon cow has got them!
Boing!
Burp! No food for you!
Spoil sport!
No buns for Star Cat!

In the morning, Dora slips back in.

Dora has a nap on Carl's bed.

Carl has food for her.

Carl's cat food is not as good as buns. But it is not too bad!